For my mum and dad —RP

For my pal Celeste, who ALWAYS has great ideas! —KD

Tundra Books, an imprint of Penguin Random House Canada Young Readers,
a division of Penguin Random House of Canada Limited

LIBRARY AND ARCHIVES CANADA CATALOGUING IN PUBLICATION

Title: How to promenade with a python (and not get eaten) / Rachel Poliquin ;
illustrated by Kathryn Durst.
Names: Poliquin, Rachel, 1975- author. | Durst, Kathryn, illustrator.
Identifiers: Canadiana (print) 20200154184 | Canadiana (ebook) 20200154206
ISBN 9780735266582 (hardcover) | ISBN 9780735266599 (EPUB)
Subjects: LCSH: Pythons—Comic books, strips, etc. | LCSH: Pythons—Juvenile literature.
LCGFT: Nonfiction comics.
Classification: LCC QL666.O67 P65 2021 | DDC j597.96/780222—dc23

Published simultaneously in the United States of America by Tundra Books of Northern New York,
an imprint of Penguin Random House Canada Young Readers,
a division of Penguin Random House of Canada Limited

LIBRARY OF CONGRESS CONTROL NUMBER: 2019956951

Edited by Elizabeth Kribs
Designed by John Martz

Special thanks to Dr. Stephen Secor and Dr. Ryan Schott for sharing their python wisdom. — RP

The artwork in this book was created using pencil crayons and finished digitally.
The text was set in set in typefaces based on hand lettering by Kathryn Durst.

PRINTED AND BOUND IN CHINA

www.penguinrandomhouse.ca

1   2   3   4   5   25 24 23 22 21

How to Promenade with a Python

(And Not Get Eaten)

RACHEL POLIQUIN

ILLUSTRATED BY KATHRYN DURST

tund

HELLO!

I'm Celeste, and I'm a
COCKROACH.

(Madagascar
Hissing
Cockroach)

Me and my kind have been around for
300 MILLION YEARS.

That's a long time.

Enough time to become experts on a great many things.
Like **SURVIVING** — I'm good at that.

But I'm not *just* a survivor. I'm a **CLASSY** survivor.

STYLISH, *Elegant,* CHIC and smart. That's me!

AND I CAN TEACH YOU.

Not just how to outsmart an ordinary

HAIRY BEAR or

SHARP-TOOTHED CAT

but how to **SURVIVE** the

POLITE PREDATORS

in your life, the sly ones that ask you to

STROLL IN THE MOONLIGHT
or HAVE TEA ON THE TERRACE.

Don't be afraid to say YES.
With my step-by-step instructions,
you'll SURVIVE
with STYLE.

TRUST ME.
I'm a classy
cockroach.
What could
POSSIBLY
go wrong?

Meet Your Predator

Let's say this is YOU,

and let's say this is a
THREE-HUNDRED-POUND
python named FRANK.

Now, I know a PROMENADE is a pleasant walk.

And you know a PYTHON
is a very large snake.

pleasant
walk
+
very large
snake
= BAD IDEA

So I'm sure we both know
that a moonlit promenade with
a python is probably a BAD IDEA.

But I like bad ideas, especially
VERY BAD IDEAS.

And right in the middle of this very bad idea are two deliciously **TRICKY PROBLEMS.**

Tricky Problem #1: Frank is slow.

A big python like Frank only moves about one mile an hour. That's faster than a snail but definitely not fast enough to promenade.

Tricky Problem #2: Frank can swallow you whole. Worse, Frank hasn't eaten for a month. And that's a problem. In fact, it's probably THE problem.

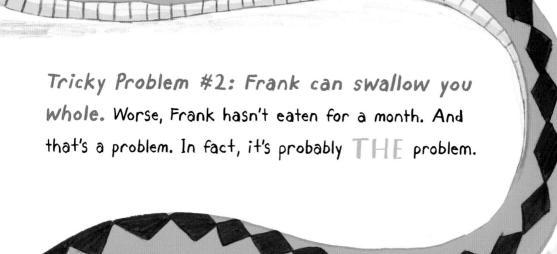

I'm beginning to think a PYTHON PROMENADE
might be the WORST idea anyone has ever had.

Problems.

PERIL.

DIFFICULTIES.

DANGER.

BAD IDEAS

I say,

"YES, PLEASE!"

So, let's you and me get down to business and
figure out how to promenade with a python
(and not get eaten).*

*Please, NEVER try any of this alone, especially if your
python asks nicely, because this is all a very, very bad idea.

STEP ONE:
Pick Your Python

There are more than forty kinds of pythons. There are spotted pythons, jungle carpet pythons, red blood pythons, white-lipped pythons, black-headed pythons and the woma, just to name a few. And I shouldn't forget the Burmese python, which is one of the five largest snakes in the world.

13

But Frank isn't just any python.
He is a RETICULATED PYTHON
(say re-TICK-q-late-tid).

And reticulated pythons grow even bigger than Burmese
pythons. Some say that the GREEN ANACONDA
(which is a boa constrictor, not a python)

is the HEAVIEST snake in the world, but everyone
says reticulated pythons are the LONGEST.

They can grow 26 feet (8 m) long and weigh 330 pounds (150 kg).
That's almost as long as a BUS and as heavy as
FOUR BABY HIPPOS.

Thankfully, most pythons — even most reticulated pythons — don't grow half as big as that.

So, IF we wanted to be safe, we COULD promenade with a smaller python. We could even ask a PYGMY PYTHON — they only grow about as long as your arm.

But where is the fun in THAT? You might as well take your cat for a walk. As my Aunty Minnie used to say,

If you're going to be a bear, be a GRIZZLY.

Besides, it's important to always consider the WORST-CASE SCENARIO. And a three-hundred-pound python named Frank is about AS BAD AS IT GETS.

KNOW YOUR PYTHON:

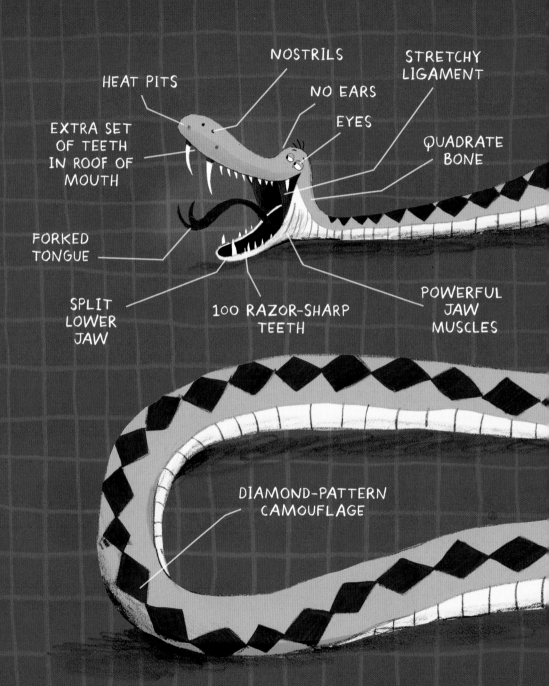

NOSTRILS

HEAT PITS

STRETCHY LIGAMENT

NO EARS

EYES

EXTRA SET OF TEETH IN ROOF OF MOUTH

QUADRATE BONE

FORKED TONGUE

SPLIT LOWER JAW

100 RAZOR-SHARP TEETH

POWERFUL JAW MUSCLES

DIAMOND-PATTERN CAMOUFLAGE

TAIL

SCALES

BELLY SCALES
(FOR LOCOMOTION)

HUNDREDS OF RIBS

STEP TWO:
Dress to Impress

A promenade isn't just a stroll —
it's more of a SHOWY PARADE.

Ladies wear their best hats,
men put flowers in their buttonholes.
Then they promenade arm in arm,
hoping everyone sees them and thinks they're
wonderfully elegant.

If you're going to promenade, you need fancier clothes.

Have you ever worn KNICKERBOCKERS?

They're short and sassy pants,
and they make anyone look smart.

(My Uncle Tony lived in a pair of
knickerbockers for years, and he
could speak three languages.)

HOLA! BONJOUR!
GUTEN TAG!

These tweedy ones should fit.

Try this hat

and this jacket.

A few final touches . . .

Now, don't you look LOVELY!

But **WHERE** is Frank? You can barely see him.

His colors and diamond patterns are perfect camouflage among those leaves. Once we get him outside, he'll just DISAPPEAR. And that won't do. Frank cannot put on a showy parade if no one can see him.

Here's what we need:

ANTI- CAMOUFLAGE PAINT.

So simple, right?

FACE PAINT

Paint a STRIPE down his back.

Maybe POLKA DOTS?
You choose. Frank won't mind.

He is mostly COLORBLIND, and his eyesight isn't the best. Just make sure you don't use browns or greens or SNEAKY jungle patterns — we want Frank to stand out, not blend in.

READY?

Oh dear. Frank **really** is
TOO SLOW.

Not to fear —
I have a plan!

Z Z Z Z Z Z

STEP THREE:
Speed Frank Up

Most snakes wriggle from side to side in a wavy motion.
Some snakes are SUPER-SPEEDY, especially in water.

But on land, big, fat snakes like Frank slowly creep forward
by rhythmically squeezing, pushing and lifting belly muscles
all along their body, sort of like a caterpillar. His large
belly scales help grip the ground as he moves forward.

Scientists call it RECTILINEAR motion
(say WRECK-tea-lynn-knee-ur).

It's very smooth and elegant, but very,
VERY slow. You probably walk three times
faster than Frank's top speed.

So, here's my idea . . .

ROLLER SKATES!

I'll admit my cousin Judy told me this was a
BAD IDEA.

She knew a python from the circus, and she said pythons
push down and lift each of their belly scales individually, as
if they were walking on HUNDREDS OF TINY
FEET. (Did I already say that pythons have one
belly scale for each rib?)

That means Frank would need one tiny skate for each of his
belly scales. And even if we found hundreds of tiny roller
skates, she said Frank might roll BACKWARD.

But roller skates are

MY FIRST AND
BEST IDEA,

so I think we should give them a try.
What's the worst that can happen?

Besides, Frank might
enjoy roller skating.
He MIGHT learn to
TWIRL and
PIROUETTE.
And I don't want
to miss that.

So, here's what we need to do:

1. MEASURE PYTHON.

Frank's body is **23 FEET LONG** (7 m).

He doesn't need a skate on his head or tail*, but he'll need one skate every 24 inches (61 cm) along his body, just so his belly doesn't rub the ground between skates.

*You can tell Frank's tail from the rest of his body because his tail doesn't have ribs or belly scales.

2. LIFT PYTHON.

Frank weighs **300 POUNDS** (136 kg).
Even a small section might weigh
more than you can lift.

I'd help
if I could.
But I'm just
a wee cockroach.

31

3. ATTACH SKATES TO PYTHON.

Frank is 35 inches (89 cm) around, far too big for the skate's buckle. Use these beautiful ribbons. They'll add a splash of style.

Hmmm . . . this is taking so long! I'm beginning to wonder why Frank asked you to promenade, when he obviously can't on his own.

Do you know what a RUSE is?
It's a trap, a scam, a piece of
PYTHON TRICKERY.

The more I think about it, the more I think maybe Frank doesn't really want to promenade.

Maybe Frank is just
HUNGRY.

DON'T PANIC!

I'm not saying he IS hungry, but pythons are sneaky.
Particularly the big ones — very, VERY sneaky.

Trust me,
NEVER TRUST
a big python like Frank.

Tell Frank you need another ribbon,
then back away, slowly.

STEP FOUR:
Know the Attack

I have good news and bad news.

The good news is that pythons are non-venomous, which means even if Frank bites you with his 100 pointy teeth, you PROBABLY won't die.

NON-VENOMOUS
FANGS

The bad news is that pythons are
CONSTRICTORS,
which means they are expert squeezers.
And you will most certainly die if Frank
gives you one of his expert squeezes.
In fact, everything Frank has ever eaten
died from one of his expert squeezes.

Obviously, Frank has to catch you
before he can squeeze you, but don't
think you're safe because Frank is slow.
Frank has caught all sorts of
superfast animals like
rabbits, birds and
monkeys.

EXPERT
SQUEEZER

TOO   TE

You see, pythons are

AMBUSH
PREDATORS,

which means they don't catch dinner
by being fast. They catch dinner
by being SNEAKY.

I'll use Mr. Jingles to explain.

1. THE AMBUSH:

Frank uses his perfect camouflage to hide among the trees and leaves until **DINNER** comes along.

TREES & LEAVES

FORWARD CREEPING MOTION

MR. JINGLES

FRANK (CAMOUFLAGED)

If he isn't close enough, he'll silently creep forward until he is near enough to strike.

(Rectilinear motion is almost completely silent, which is very good for Frank but very bad for everyone else.)

2. THE STRIKE:

Once Frank is in perfect strike position,
QUICK AS A FLASH, he lunges and bites
dinner, usually on the back of the neck,
so dinner can't fight back.

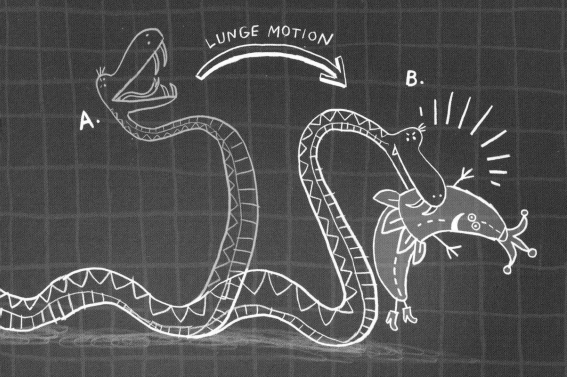

LUNGE MOTION

A.

B.

Frank's 100 sharp and pointy teeth are recurved,
which means they curve backward toward his throat.
And that means **NOTHING** escapes Frank's bite.

3. THE WRAP:

Using the speed and momentum of the strike, Frank throws himself around dinner's body. In less than a second, he is wrapped three times around.

4. THE SQUEEZE:

Frank squeezes **TIGHTER AND TIGHTER**
with muscles all along his body.

He squeezes until dinner's heart can't pump.
He squeezes until dinner can't breathe.
Frank squeezes until dinner is dead, and he continues to

SQUEEZE AND SQUEEZE

just to be sure.

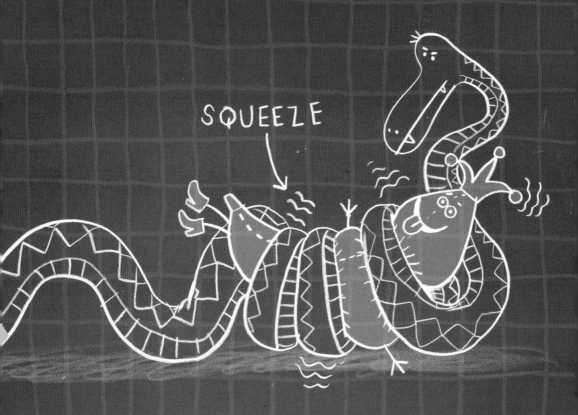

SQUEEZE

5. THE SWALLOW:

Frank starts with the head
and swallows dinner whole.
Awful, isn't it?
Just **AWFUL** and **TERRIBLE.**

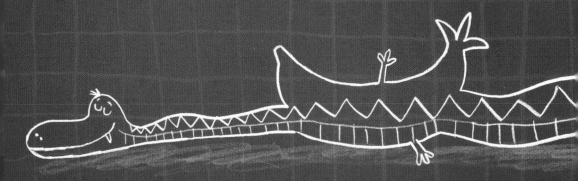

BUT SURPRISINGLY TIDY!

When lions and hyenas tear into their dinners,
they spatter blood and gore everywhere.
Instead, Frank slowly and cleanly gulps dinner down,
without chewing or tearing a single bite.

But still, awful. Just AWFUL
and TERRIBLE.

Especially if it happened to YOU.

Tie this **BELL** onto Frank's tail — that will stop him from sneaking around.

Now, let's make sure you don't get **SWALLOWED WHOLE.**

STEP FIVE:
Get a Bigger Head

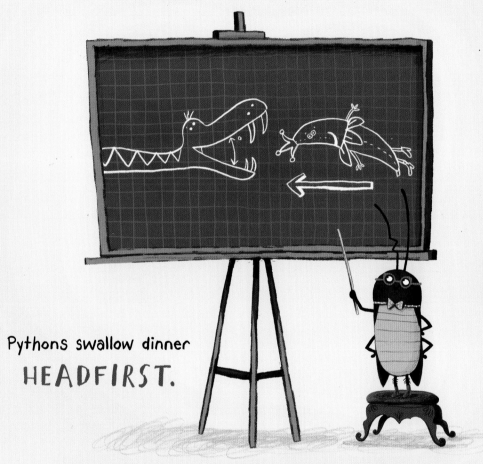

Pythons swallow dinner
HEADFIRST.

That's because heads are usually an animal's smallest part. Also, fur, feathers, arms, legs and poke-y things like Mr. Jingles's shoes lie flat when going down the throat that way.

If your head is wider than Frank's jaws, you should be safe.
But don't be fooled by the size of Frank's mouth.

MR. JINGLES is skinnier than Frank, which makes
for an easy swallow. But Frank can eat all sorts of lumpy
meals like PIGS and MONKEYS

and . . . well . . . YOU.

In fact, Frank can swallow meals up to
THREE TIMES WIDER
than his head and body.

You wouldn't think he could do it.
But pythons aren't built like you.

FOR STARTERS, Frank has super elastic
skin, and his scales are only attached on one side
for extra stretch. Also, his ribs aren't joined at the
front like yours, so his entire body can swell to fit
a particularly bulgy meal. Impressive, right?

BUT WAIT UNTIL YOU HEAR
WHAT HIS HEAD CAN DO!

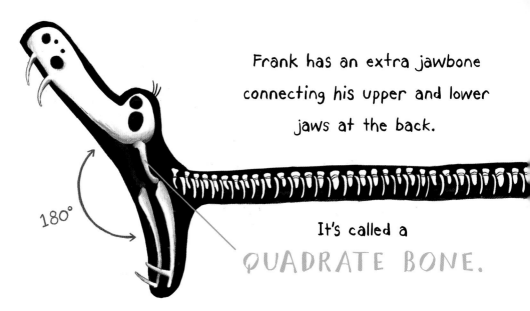

Frank has an extra jawbone connecting his upper and lower jaws at the back.

180°

It's called a

QUADRATE BONE.

It works like a double-jointed hinge so Frank can open his mouth 180 degrees wide. And THAT, I'm afraid, is most DEFINITELY wide enough to fit your head.

Next, Frank's lower jaw is actually two pieces held together by a stretchy bit at the front, so his whole mouth can expand sideways.

Frank even has an extra set of teeth on the roof of his mouth to help grab and drag dinner down his throat. All of this means Frank could swallow you as easy as a

CHOCOLATE-
DIPPED ÉCLAIR.

Here's what I'm thinking:

A LAMPSHADE.

Wear it as a hat!

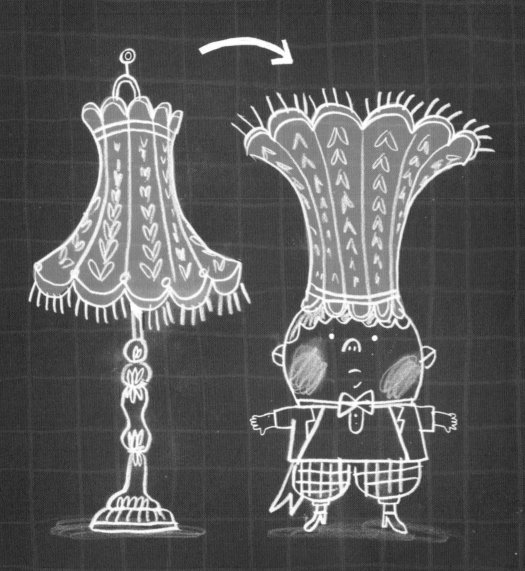

If you turn it upside down, Frank will
NEVER get his mouth around it.

That lampshade is beautiful and
way too big for Frank's mouth.
But we have a serious problem.
You look RIDICULOUS,
not wonderfully elegant at all!

Worse, Frank can still SQUEEZE
you dead in the body.

But if we can stop the
SQUEEZE,
we don't have to
worry about the
SWALLOW.

How clever am I?

STEP SIX:
Build an Anti-Squeeze Shield

I've got a few anti-squeeze shield ideas we could try.

THREE INNER TUBES

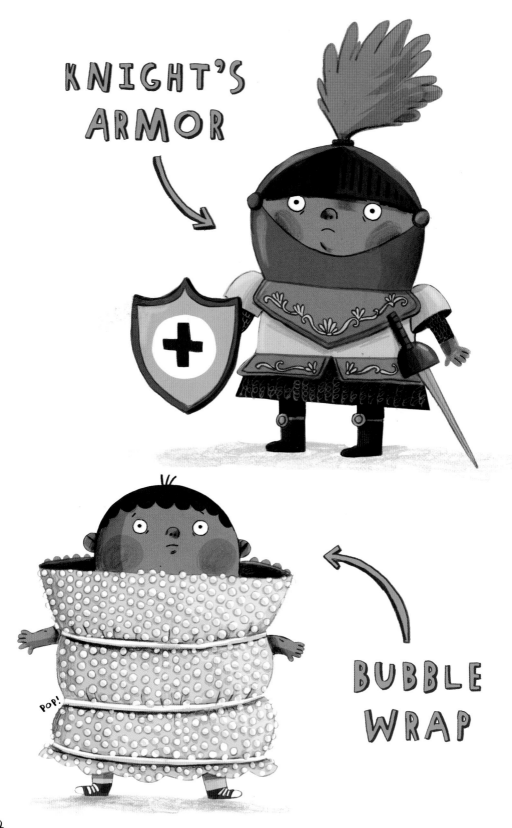

KNIGHT'S
ARMOR

BUBBLE
WRAP

POP!

Well, the good news is that your neck is covered. Necks are Frank's favorite things to bite. I know I said his bite *probably* won't kill you, but a 100-tooth bite is plain NASTY.

The bad news is that I'm just remembering pythons have one of the most POWERFUL SQUEEZES in the animal kingdom. He'll squash those inner tubes like crumpets. He'll crush the armor like a fine Ming vase. Bubble wrap doesn't stand a chance. These anti-squeeze shields aren't going to work AT ALL.

Let me think . . .
Let me think . . .

POP!

AHA!

I have another brilliant idea! If Frank can't find you, he can't bite you! **RIGHT?!** I'm a GENIUS!

All we need to do is make you

INVISIBLE.

And I know exactly how to do it.

STEP SEVEN:
Freeze Your Pants

Reticulated pythons are mostly

NOCTURNAL,

which means they mostly hunt at night.

(That's why Frank asked you for

a *moonlit* promenade.)

To hunt at night, Frank needs good

NIGHT VISION

and a great

SENSE OF SMELL,

which he has.

SNIFF
SNIFF
SNIFF

But Frank also has

SPECIAL PYTHON POWERS

for finding dinner in the dark.

You see, Frank likes to eat
HOT-BLOODED animals
such as mammals and birds.
(You're hot-blooded, too.)

At night, animal bodies can be much hotter than the cooler air. And when that happens, Frank can "**see**" the heat of an animal's body. Not with his eyes but with a row of tiny holes on his face called **HEAT PITS.**

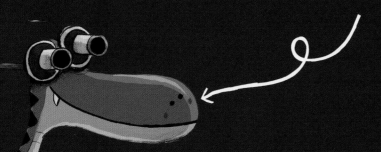

Heat pits work like
NIGHT-VISION GOGGLES
and let Frank see animal heat
even in pitch-black
DARKNESS.

So here's the plan: to make you invisible to Frank, we just need to make you **COLDER THAN THE AIR.** Then turn off the lights. You and Frank can promenade all night, and he'll never know you're there!

CHATTER
CHATTER

1. Soak knickerbockers, woolly hat, socks and mittens in icy water.

ICE

2. Freeze the clothes.

3. Put on frozen clothes.

If we place this thermometer under your tongue, we can use this other one to compare to the air temperature.

4. Turn off the light . . .

Don't worry. We cockroaches have the best night vision around. I'll be right here on your shoulder to keep an eye on Frank.

STOP SHIVERING!
Shivering is how hot-blooded animals warm themselves up. Think TOASTY thoughts.

AND WHAT'S THAT NOISE?

Your teeth are chattering? That's a problem.
Snakes don't have ears, so Frank can't
HEAR your chattering, but he can FEEL
the vibrations through his entire body.

With all that shaking and chattering,
Frank knows EXACTLY
where you are.

BUT WHERE IS FRANK?
I can't see him anywhere.
How can a three-hundred-pound
python just disappear?!

If Frank tries to bite you,
he might skewer ME by accident.

Was that his bell?

DANGER!

PERIL!

This is a
NO-GOOD-VERY-BAD
PLAN!

TURN ON THE LIGHTS!

TURN ON
THE LIGHTS!

65

Don't look at me like that.

I did warn you that I like very bad ideas.
But now I have an ESPECIALLY good one.

PROMISE.

STEP EIGHT:
Give Your Python a Snack

Why didn't I think of this earlier?
If Frank has a snack, he PROBABLY won't eat you.

It shouldn't be too little, but it can't be too big either.
Too little (like a mouse) and Frank would still be
hungry. Too big (like a pig) would be worse.
The last pig Frank ate took him over an hour
to swallow, and a whole week to digest.

And while he was
digesting, Frank just
wanted to lie in a
warm place, large
and lumpy like a log.
I don't have time to
wait around for that.

Here's the plan: we feed Frank a chicken.
I'm sorry to say this, but the chicken needs to be alive
or Frank won't eat it — Frank won't eat a cold dinner.

And YOU'LL have to do it.
Because that chicken may
try to eat me.
We wouldn't want
THAT.

IT'S TOO GRUESOME!

I can't watch. I'll close my eyes.
Tell me when Frank's finished.

WHAT THE — !?

HEY! Where are you going?

THAT'S TOO FAST FOR A PROMENADE!

WAIT FOR ME!!

THE END

WHEW!
THAT WAS A CLOSE ONE!

I hope you'll join me again next time a
polite predator invites you to tea on the terrrace
or a polka in the park. With me at your side,

WHAT COULD POSSIBLY
GO WRONG?

RACHEL POLIQUIN writes about animals, mostly. She has written about ostriches, sled dogs, heroic moles and 800,000 jars of pickled fish. She is the author of *Beastly Puzzles: A Brain-Boggling Animal Guessing Game* and the *Superpower Field Guide* series. She lives in Vancouver, Canada, with her husband and three children.

KATHRYN DURST has illustrated numerous children's books, including the #1 *New York Times* bestseller from Paul McCartney, *Hey Grandude!* When she is not illustrating books, she can be found playing the accordion, growing vegetables, folk dancing or putting on shadow puppet shows. She lives in Toronto, Canada, with her grumpy mini dachshund named Chili Dog.